Catskill Creatures

by
Nancy Furstinger

Illustrations by
Bob Ebdon

golden
NOTE
BOOK
PRESS
WOODSTOCK, NY

Dedicated to my sweet guy and fellow animal aficionado Gary Hoeting—
I've loved you ever since I carved GH on my garage wall as a kid—N.F.

To Gillian—B.E.

Catskill Creatures

First published in 2024 by Golden Notebook Press
Copyright © by Nancy Furstinger

All rights reserved.

First Golden Notebook Printing: January 2024

Golden Notebook Press, LLC
29 Tinker Street
Woodstock, NY 12498

goldennotebook.com
goldennotebookpress.com
@goldennotebookbookstore

ISBN: 978-0-9675541-6-7

Designed by James Conrad

Printed in the United States of America
1 3 5 7 9 10 8 6 4 2

First Edition

Table of Contents

Our task must be to free ourselves by widening our circle of compassion to embrace all living creatures and the whole of nature in its beauty.

—ALBERT EINSTEIN

In the end, we will conserve only what we love; we will love only what we understand and we will understand only what we are taught.

—BABA DIOUM

We need another and a wiser and perhaps a more mystical concept of animals. Remote from universal nature, and living by complicated artifice, man in civilization surveys the creature through the glass of his knowledge and sees thereby a feather magnified and the whole image in distortion. We patronize them for their incompleteness, for their tragic fate of having taken form so far below ourselves. And therein we err, and greatly err. For the animal shall not be measured by man. In a world older and more complete than ours they move finished and complete, gifted with extensions of the senses we have lost or never attained, living by voices we shall never hear. They are not brethren, they are not underlings; they are other nations, caught with ourselves in the net of life and time, fellow prisoners of the splendor and travail of the earth.

—HENRY BESTON
The Outermost House

Introduction

IF YOU'RE LUCKY ENOUGH TO LIVE IN or visit the Catskill Mountains in New York, you can watch wonderful creatures who crawl, walk, run, swim, slither, hop, and fly right through your backyard. Each has a fascinating story to tell.

Where else can you discover how coyotes howl to communicate, why black bears scratch trees, what stinky snack great horned owls enjoy, who benefits by bats, and when wood frogs freeze solid? In the Catskills, nature's outdoor theater offers a new drama each season, and the animals are the stars!

You can learn more about your wild neighbors and their habitats by quietly and patiently observing them. Stay motionless and hidden behind shrubs or trees. Watch bluebirds build nests through binoculars. Capture a squirrel ballet on your camera. Record the great horned owl's hoot. Sketch skunks from afar. Write about the antics of raccoons. Track foxes through the snow.

Enjoy wild creatures in the great outdoors, but don't be tempted to transform one into a pet. Remember, only nature provides the perfect environment for each creature's survival.

After reading about the 15 Catskill creatures spotlighted in this book, make your neighborhood wildlife friendly by following the suggestions in the "How You Can Help" section.

Beaver

BEAVERS, THE OFFICIAL MAMMAL OF NEW YORK, are nature's conservationists. When they dam small streams, beavers create ponds that hold large amounts of water from rain and melting snow. The water flows slowly, preventing flooding and soil erosion. Beavers forge a special setting that welcomes water creatures, birds, and thirsty animals.

These master builders use teeth and paws to construct dams, lodges, and storehouses. Generations of beavers can build a 1,000-foot-long dam. First they gnaw down trees and float them to a shallow spot in the stream. Then beavers bury an end of the branches in mud and add stones for strength. A dome-shaped lodge with an above-water platform and underwater entrances offers a cozy spot safe from predators.

As the largest rodents in North America, weighing up to 60 pounds, beavers are designed for swimming and chewing. Reddish brown fur and a lush undercoat guarantee that beavers will be warm and waterproof when they swim in icy Catskill waters. Webbed hind feet and paddle-shaped tails propel them through water. Their tails prop beavers upright while sitting and warn of danger when slapped down loudly in the water. Beaver noses contain valves that close when diving underwater—up to a total of 15 minutes! Enormous orange teeth, which constantly grow, act as a sharp chisel to fell trees.

Beavers live in a family colony. Males and females often mate for life. Each autumn they fatten up for the coming winter and gather branches for their underwater storehouse. Fresh green bark from poplar, willow, and birch trees forms their winter diet.

After a winter's rest, one to eight kits are born in the spring. Fully furred and with eyes wide open, the baby beavers will swim within one month.

Big and Little Brown Bat

MILLIONS OF YEARS AGO, bats soared among the dinosaurs. Today's bats keep the same schedule, swooping out at dusk and disappearing at dawn.

Bats are the only flying mammals. Wings of elastic skin spread out from the sides of their furry bodies. Bats can fly in total darkness by using echolocation. They bounce sounds off of nearby objects. Then they judge distances by the time required for the echo to return. Big brown bats zoom through the Catskills at speeds up to 40 miles per hour. Their smaller relative, the little brown bat, flies between 20 to 30 mph.

Bats have huge appetites. On the menu are night-flying insects such as beetles, moths, and mosquitoes. One little brown bat can gobble 1,200 insects in just an hour! Bats are nature's original bug zapper. They reduce the need for harmful pesticides.

Baby bats are born tail first. They are blind and naked. The mother bat bears usually just one baby, called a pup, each year. She hangs by her feet and thumbs, giving birth upside down.

Big and little brown bats live in tree hollows and buildings. Each winter they hibernate for up to seven months. These bats can decrease their heart rate to between ten to 20 beats per minute.

Bats gained a bad rap as evil creatures because of their appearance. However, these night-flying goblins will not suck your blood or get tangled in your hair. Never handle bats and you'll have nothing to fear.

Black Bear

BLACK BEARS LUMBER THROUGH THE CATSKILLS, shyly avoiding humans. These are bruins on a mission: filling their stomachs. Although black bears weigh 14 ounces at birth, large adult males top 600 pounds, but most average 300 pounds, twice as much as females.

Surprisingly, bears are primarily vegetarian, foraging for shoots, leaves, grasses, acorns, beechnuts, corn, berries, and wild fruits. They also have a sweet tooth, climbing trees for honey. Bears search for insect larvae beneath large stones and gobble sunflower seeds from birdfeeders.

Jet black with a brown snout, the black bear has poor vision but compensates with a superb sense of smell—50 times greater than humans. Curved claws allow the bear to climb and scratch trees to mark territory. Males stake out about 25 square miles of forested land, females about 15. If surprised by people in their habitat, most bears will race away at speeds up to 35 miles per hour.

In late September, black bears put on weight to prepare for winter, when they will lose 25 percent of their body fat. Around the end of November, a pregnant female or one with cubs heads into a small rock chamber that serves as her den. The male retreats to his own hideout, a brush pile or hollow tree, about three weeks later. Bears don't truly hibernate. Instead their body temperature drops ten degrees and they fall into a deep sleep, from which they can quickly awaken if disturbed.

In January, two to four blind and hairless cubs about the size of guinea pigs are born. Mother bears, called sows, fiercely protect their young. Cubs quickly learn to climb trees at the first hint of danger. They'll wrestle with each other and travel alongside their mother until their second spring.

Brook Trout

A Catskill trout stream can hook you with its natural, constantly changing drama. Here New York's official state fish—the brook trout—swims in clear water pulsating through streams where temperatures never rise above seventy-two degrees.

Each spring, the stream thaws and swirls to life. Mayflies and caddis flies dance over the surface. Splash! Brook trout speckled in jewel tones of red, silver, and gold leap and take flies with a snap. Most of these six- to ten-inch fish weigh less than two pounds, although an eight-and-a-half pounder caught in 1908 set a record.

Crystal springs tumbling through hills feed the trout stream, and trees surround and shade it. This creates the perfect environment for brook trout. Without the upstream springs, in the summer the stream would hardly flow. And if the water became any warmer, the brook trout would feed less and lose weight.

With the fall comes spawning season, when the trout migrate upstream to breed. The female brook trout selects a spot on the inside of a bend in the stream. At this location the water speed is slower. She builds her nest with powerful thrusts into the streambed gravel and lays her eggs in the hollow. The male jealously guards the female's nest from other suitors. He swims by the female and quickly fertilizes her eggs. In a few months, the young trout, called fry, hatch. Like clockwork, each year the trout return to their native streams to spawn.

As the first snows fall, the trout seek out winter holes where they can live in the freezing streams. Their body functions slow down. Ice forms among the rocks and the brook trout slumber, dreaming of catching flies.

Coyote

A SERIES OF HIGH-PITCHED YELPS followed by a long, eerie howl echo throughout the Catskills. With this ghostly evening concert, coyotes vocalize their locations. Most prefer to live alone or with their mates, but some juvenile coyotes form small packs. These adaptable animals have expanded their range throughout North America, surviving in a variety of habitats.

A member of the canine family, the coyote is about the size of a young German shepherd dog, weighing an average of 35 pounds. Thick tawny-gray fur protects them from the elements. Like dogs, coyotes' long pointed noses can sniff out prey and their pricked ears pick up faraway sounds. However, unlike dogs, coyotes carry their bushy tails low as they run. Their tracks differ also—to conserve energy, coyotes will place their back feet into the prints made by the front feet.

As predators, coyotes stalk and pounce upon small prey such as mice, squirrels, turkey, and rabbits. Groups of coyotes join together and race at speeds up to 43 mph to hunt larger animals like deer. They also enjoy a buffet of fish, reptiles, insects such as grasshoppers, fruits, and trash.

Pairs of coyotes are believed to mate for life. After choosing a partner, the couple builds a den, digging out a tunnel and nursery. In the spring, four to ten fully furred but blind pups are born. Both parents raise the pups, regurgitating meat to feed them and teaching hunting skills.

In autumn the young coyotes are driven from their parents' territory to search for their own food supply. They will travel up to 100 miles to claim their own area, where each will sing a solo chorus!

Eastern American Toad

WITH THEIR SUPER WARTY DRY SKIN, flexible tongues, knobby feet, and curious trilling sounds, eastern American toads could have arrived from another planet. These traits, however, serve fascinating—and earthly—purposes.

Toads range in color from reddish brown to olive, with black spots. Each spot contains one or two warts that secrete a sticky white substance. While the stuff makes many predators who bite toads ill, it will not cause warts in humans. Despite the danger, raccoons, owls, and skunks dine on toads without getting stomachaches.

Toads capture and gobble insects, earthworms, beetles, slugs, and spiders with their long elastic tongues. Buggy eyes help these amphibians catch their supper.

Gardens and damp woodlands across the Catskills conceal toads. Here they use special knobs on their hind feet to shove soil aside until they sink into underground burrows. These amphibians are cold-blooded creatures—their body temperature changes with the weather. To survive winter, toads bury themselves as deep as three feet into the soil.

When male toads come out of hibernation, they hop over to shallow ponds. Many return to the same ponds each spring, finding their way back by smell and the position of the stars. Here their chorus of long, musical trills attracts female toads.

Soon the female will lay two strings with up to 12,000 eggs protected in a jellylike coating. Then tiny black tadpoles hatch in shallow water, where they start swimming. Tadpoles look more like fish with tails and gills to breathe underwater. In about three months they transform into toads. Soon the tail disappears as legs appear and gills change into lungs.

Eastern Bluebird

"SOMEWHERE OVER THE RAINBOW, BLUEBIRDS FLY." The colorful songbirds in the song nearly vanished into the Land of Oz due to habitat loss. When trees were bulldozed for developments, and metal posts replaced wooden fences where bluebirds nested, a housing shortage occurred. Bluebird fans raced to the rescue, hammering and mounting nesting boxes. Some created bluebird trails—a series of five or more boxes along routes.

The eastern bluebird is New York's official state bird. Nesting locations include open rural country with scattered trees, such as pastures, cemeteries, and golf courses. This makes the Catskills prime real estate! Birders mount wooden nesting boxes with one-and-a-half-inch entrance holes five feet up on pipe poles.

One of the first birds to return North in spring, bluebirds nest and hatch in the Catskill area during May and June. They weave grass and pine needles into a cup-shaped nest. The female lays one light blue egg each day before noon. She waits until after laying all her eggs, usually four or five, before incubating them. They hatch in approximately two weeks. Nestlings fledge, or fly from the nest, when they're about three weeks old. Young from the first brood might return to help parents raise a second flock.

Eastern bluebirds carry the colors of the sunset: brilliant sky blue feathers with rusty breasts and white bellies. Males have brighter plumage than females.

Wild berries along with insects, such as crickets and grasshoppers, are on the menu. Bluebirds can eat on the run, catching flying insects in midair. If invited, these birds gobble mealworms from neighborhood feeders.

Eastern Cotton-Tailed Rabbit

ONE PAIR OF EASTERN COTTON-TAILED RABBITS could create their own Catskill kingdom. The female rabbit, or doe, gives birth to two or three litters each season. Three to eight baby bunnies are in every batch. Those born in the spring can start families in the autumn. At the end of five years, that one pair of rabbits could multiply into two-and-a-half million!

The mother rabbit builds a nest. She plucks hair from her belly and mixes it with leaves. Baby rabbits are born blind, naked, and unable to hop. After the first week, their ears and eyes open. The rabbits grow grayish-buff fur with a white belly. Their cottony tails look like powder puffs.

Soon the rabbits scamper off. They spend much of the day concealing themselves from danger in forms—hollows scratched out under grasses or brush piles. In unusually cold weather, cotton-tailed rabbits live underground in burrows at forest borders or in fields. Since rabbits prefer to leave the excavation to other creatures, they usually rent abandoned woodchuck burrows.

Rabbits surface from sunset to sunrise. They nibble green plants, bark, buds, and grasses. Brave bunnies might hop into your garden, searching for leafy greens and other vegetables.

Many enemies stalk rabbits. They hide from predators such as foxes, hawks, and snakes during the day. If a hungry enemy approaches, the rabbit freezes. Any closer and the rabbit zigzags in speeds up to 18 miles per hour.

Rabbits have built-in radar. Their ears swivel to detect danger from all directions. Their big brown eyes bulge. Rabbits can see over their shoulders without turning their heads. Wiggly noses capture airborne scents. Rabbits' large hind feet stamp out a warning and allow them to escape with eight-foot leaps.

Gray and Red Fox

FOXES HAVE EARNED THEIR SLY REPUTATION. They cleverly avoid capture by retracing their tracks and leaping sideways, swimming across a stream, or running atop a stone wall!

And foxes also use clever tricks to fill their belly. If they spot a duck splashing in a pond, foxes frolic on shore. Becoming curious, the duck paddles closer to investigate. Pounce—cunning foxes will have their dinner! Using another capture trick, foxes will leap three feet into the air and dive, front paws first, onto rodents.

Both red and gray foxes, often mistaken for each other, belong to the canine family. Although born gray, red foxes soon sport reddish-golden fur, a white bib and tail tip, and black feet. Their gray cousins are a silvery shade with a black muzzle and patches of bright reddish-orange on the neck and chest.

Besides ducks and mice, both foxes feed on birds, small mammals, eggs, acorns, grasshoppers, crickets, fish, and fruit. Only gray foxes are capable of climbing trees to escape from danger or snack on fruits. Using long claws to scurry up and down, they'll also ambush roosting birds from their aerial perch.

On ground, the forests, streams, and open fields of the Catskills offer prime places for fox dens. They tunnel beneath boulders, in hollow logs, caves, or empty burrows. Shredded bark and leaves line nests. Here the male dog fox and female vixen raise their litter of about five baby cubs each spring.

The fox parents and their young are territorial, marking boundaries by leaving scent "messages." They also warn intruders with yapping barks and shrill howls.

Gray and Red Squirrel

TREE SQUIRRELS ARE THE ACROBATS OF THE CATSKILLS, balancing on high wires and leaping though treetops. Their backyard antics amuse nature watchers.

Eastern gray squirrels spend most of their time gathering and gobbling food. Favorites include nuts and seeds from trees, corn, peanuts, insects, bird eggs, and sunflower seeds. Before winter, gray squirrels busily bury nuts in separate holes. When snow covers the earth, they sniff out their underground pantry. Many buried nuts go undiscovered and germinate in the spring.

Red squirrels hoard pinecones, nuts, and mushrooms, stashing them in hollow trees and stone walls. In winter they tunnel through the snow to their supplies.

Gray squirrels have a coat of short brown and black fur with white tips. Some sport totally black coats; rarer are white albinos with pink eyes. Bushy tails as long as their bodies, about ten inches, serve triple duty as umbrellas, quilts, and balancing poles. Gray squirrels communicate danger by waving their tails and making high-pitched scolding and barking sounds. Their bright red cousins chatter and stamp their feet. Although smaller, red squirrels will chase and fight gangs of gray squirrels.

Friendly families of gray squirrels share sky top nests of leaves and twigs in the highest branches of the tallest trees. Up there, squirrels sleep, seek shelter from storms, and start families. Solitary red squirrels build nests in tree hollows, burrows, or even attics. A litter of three to five baby squirrels, born in late winter or spring, is protected by the mother until their eyes open.

Great Horned Owl

GREAT HORNED OWLS OBVIOUSLY have a stinky sense of smell since their favorite snacks are skunks! They make up for it with extremely sensitive eyes and ears, designed to help them navigate the night. As the large bright yellow eyes only face forward, owls must turn their heads to keep prey in sight. They can rotate their heads 270 degrees to see sideways. Earlike tufts of feathers called horns appear on each side of the rounded head.

Soft dark brown feathers banded with black cover the great horned owl's body. A white throat collar appears below the flattened face. The owl's flight is almost noiseless thanks to downy plumage. Huge wings span from 36 to 60 inches, making this bird one of the largest and most powerful American owls.

Once owls detect prey, they'll soar down for the kill, using strong talons and hooked bills. Owls swallow their victims whole, and then regurgitate bones, feathers, and fur as pellets. A close examination of these reveals the meal: birds, fish, reptiles, and mammals such as rodents, rabbits, and skunks.

This majestic bird lives in many types of Catskill habitats, from forests to cemeteries. Most do not migrate. Pairs nest in tree holes, cliff ledges, caves, or on the ground. Owls use old nests from other large birds or squirrels instead of building their own. They nest in late winter, keeping eggs warm during snowstorms! After hatching from the two to three eggs laid in winter, owlets spend up to two weeks in the nest. Soon they fly off on their own adventures.

At nightfall great horned owls can be heard calling to each other. Sounds range from cackling to hooting.

RNE

Raccoon

CLEVER RACCOONS CAN CREATE MISCHIEF using their almost human front paws. They quickly learn how to open doors, turn on faucets, and pry off garbage can lids during midnight raids. Before they gorge on the trashy treats, raccoons will sometimes wash both the food and their paws. They enjoy playing with their meals! It appears these mammals will eat anything, including fish, frogs, turtles, mice, insects, fruit, vegetables, honey, and nuts.

Raccoons are fond of snacking, and their plump bodies can tip the scales at up to 30 pounds. They sport salt and pepper fur with a trademark black face mask. Black bands circle their bushy ringtails.

These masked bandits are right at home in the Catskills. Prime raccoon real estate features wooded areas near water. A hollow tree cavity provides shelter and a place to curl up for a long winter's sleep. Raccoons don't actually hibernate, although they do slow down when snow season begins. They're most active at night, but some will stroll out in the sunlight, especially mothers foraging for food.

In the spring, three to four babies, called kits or cubs, are born. Lightly furred, they have faint masks and both their eyes and ears are closed. Baby raccoons make a variety of sounds, including growling, purring, churring, and trilling. At first they crawl like furry spiders, but when kits are about six weeks old they begin to explore by walking, running, and climbing. They wouldn't win any races, waddling like a bear. However, 20 sharp claws help raccoons climb up and down trees rapidly.

Soon the babies wrestle with their brothers and sisters, pretending they're predators. Enemies include coyotes, bobcats, foxes, and owls. Babies stay with their mothers for up to a year, learning raccoon survival tricks.

Skunk

THE STRIPED SKUNK'S LATIN NAME, Mephitis mephitis, translates into "stinks stinks." If you've gotten close to one, you'll know why the word is repeated. This mammal manufactures a potent defense weapon—a smelly liquid that temporarily blinds enemies.

Skunks always growl and stamp their feet in warning before spraying. If the intruder comes closer, skunks raise their tails, but the white tip hangs down. One step closer, and up goes the tip as skunks takes aim. Quick, escape before they fire two jets of liquid spray that can travel up to 12 feet! Skunks discharge five or six shots with deadly accuracy.

Skunks don't have many enemies willing to challenge such odorous opponents. Great horned owls have a poor sense of smell, allowing them to turn the skunk into a meal without getting contaminated.

Striped skunks live only in North America. Their Catskill habitat includes forest borders and grassy fields. Skunks drag dried leaves and grass into their dens to make a mat. In winter, balls of grass pushed into the entranceway block out the cold. Skunks don't hibernate, but take long naps.

About the size of a house cat, skunks sport black coats with two white stripes down the back and one up the forehead. Baby skunks are bald, blind, and toothless. A litter of four to eight babies, called kittens, is ready to hunt in two months. Skunks forage at night, chowing down on insects, fruits, roots and leaves, and small rodents and reptiles. They're excellent mousers just like many cats.

White-Tailed Deer

WHITE-TAILED DEER BOUND ACROSS Catskill meadows, gracefully leaping at heights of more than eight feet. The herd flashes their trademark white tails like warning flags. Sharp senses of hearing and smell help deer to avoid predators of the two- and four-legged variety. After detecting an enemy, deer will stamp their feet and make a loud snorting sound before racing off at speeds of up to 45 miles per hour.

Timid males, or bucks, transform into fierce warriors during autumn mating season. Contestants clash their spiked antlers in contests of strength. Antlers begin as tiny buds. As they grow, antlers are covered with velvet, which the buck rubs off on trees, advertising his presence. Each year bucks shed and then grow a larger set branched with tines, or "points," that increase with age.

In spring, females, or does, give birth to one or two fawns. White speckles dappled on reddish coats keep fawns camouflaged in their sunlight beds of leaves. Since they have no scent at first, fawns are safe from enemies such as black bears and coyotes. Does disappear to feed, returning often to nurse their babies.

White-tailed deer graze at sunset and sunrise in old fields, woodland clearings, and orchards. In summer, they munch on grasses and other herbs; in winter they browse on twigs and bark of trees and bushes. Favorite treats include corn and wild apples. Like their diets, these creatures' coats change with the season. A red summer coat of fine hairs turns into a gray winter coat with hollow hairs that insulate against frosty weather.

Wood Frog

WOOD FROGS HAVE A SECRET FORMULA for surviving freezing Catskill weather. Their liver produces glycerol, a sweet, syrupy alcohol that acts as antifreeze, as soon as temperatures drop. These creatures bury themselves in the woodlands and transform into ice sculptures. As long as the ground is below freezing, wood frogs have the amazing ability to freeze solid while still alive!

Coming out of the deep freeze, their heart begins beating and lungs fill with air. Wood frogs awaken from their icy slumber and thaw. Then they hop off to the nearest pond or puddle in early spring. There they croak their special song—a hoarse quacking tune—to attract females. These fellas are in a rush since wood frogs breed for only three or four nights each year.

Female wood frogs lay clusters of eggs so small that dozens could fit in a tablespoon. A single cluster can contain 2,000 eggs. In about three weeks tadpoles hatch. Those that survive snakes and birds sprout legs in eight to ten weeks. Soon the body reabsorbs the tail, and the froglet leaves the pond for a forested area.

Wood frogs are never far from moisture, however, because their smooth, slippery skin is in constant danger of drying up. Coloring varies from light tan to dark brown, with a dark mask around their bulging eyes. Long and strong webbed hind feet help wood frogs leap and swim.

When wood frogs spot a tasty insect such as a dragonfly, they rapidly roll out tongues resembling upside-down birthday party horns. Snap—their long, sticky tongues seize the bug. The frogs' eyes close and sink into their heads as they swallow. Wood frogs apply pressure to their eyeballs to help shove a meal down their throats!

How You Can Help

You can help protect our Catskills.
These tips will make it a cleaner greener spot for all creatures.

- Beaver ponds create wetlands that become magnets for wildlife. Install flow devices for an environmentally friendly way to control water levels at dams and prevent flooding problems. Protect trees from gnawing with wire cylinders.

- Bats contribute to a healthy environment, but many are being forced out of their forest habitats. Make sure these shy, fascinating creatures don't disappear. You can mount a bat house on a pole so they have a safe spot to roost.

- Respect bears from far distances. Feeding bears is against the law and endangers them. Ensure that bears don't become problematic by securing garbage cans inside and removing birdseed feeders in the summer.

- Pollution and habitat destruction threaten brook trout, along with the introduction of non-native fish species. When you hike along a stream, pick up trash, especially discarded fishing lines and hooks.

- Coyotes play an essential role in keeping our ecosystem healthy and balanced. Sometimes you can communicate long-distance with wild coyotes. Imitate their two short barks and a long yodel. Perhaps they'll answer back!

- Greedy gobblers of insects, toads need wetlands to survive. Toads are unable to create tadpoles if their pond is drained or polluted. Encourage a toad to move into your yard by providing an upside-down flowerpot for shelter.

- Add color and motion to your yard by attracting bluebirds. Nail a board into a tree stump. Then fill this platform feeder with rose hips, dogwood berries, sunflower seeds, raisins soaked in water, and a plastic tub of mealworms.

- Rabbits need safe spots to hide from enemies. Provide brush piles to offer protection. Plant clover, alfalfa, and wild grasses so they can graze. Check your yard for nests before mowing and keep pet dogs and cats away.

- Fur-bearing mammals such as foxes have long been hunted and trapped for their pelts. The only one who can wear a fur coat with grace and beauty is the animal born with it. Boycott fur!

- Squirrels keep forests healthy by helping sprout new trees. Distract these feisty furballs from raiding your bird feeder by filling a tray with an assortment of goodies: cracked corn, peanuts, sunflower seeds, pumpkin seeds, and millet.

- Take a nighttime nature walk to search for great horned owls. Imitate owls' calls—five whos followed by a long whooooooo—and wait for their reply. If you shine a flashlight into the treetops, the birds might soar past you.

- Cap chimneys and check for nests of raccoons before starting that first fire. Feed pets indoors and keep pet doors closed at night to keep curious raccoons in the wild where they belong.

- If your inquisitive dog gets doused by a skunk's pungent perfume, mix up this shampoo: 1 quart of 3% hydrogen peroxide, 1/4 cup baking soda, and 1 teaspoon liquid dishwashing soap. Don't store this mixture: it could explode.

- Encourage your neighborhood to mount reflectors along the roadside to reduce deer-vehicle collisions. These devices reflect car headlights and create an optical illusion of a fence and warn deer of oncoming cars.

- Wood frogs face threats from pollution and loss of wetland habitats. Join with others to clean up waterways or build a backyard pond for neighborhood frogs. And don't dissect frogs in your classroom—use a 3-D anatomy model instead.

Nature's Superheroes

Imagine you spot a bear cub tumbling out of a tree.
Or perhaps your dog digs up a nest of cottontail bunnies.
Or maybe a great horned owlet slams into a window.
Who should you call when animals need help?

Fortunately, many wildlife rehabilitators are on call 24/7 in the Catskills. These rehabbers are nature's superheroes. Their superpowers include rescuing sick, injured, and orphaned animals; providing medical care, and nursing them back to health. Then rehabilitators release most wildlife back into the wild where they gain a second chance at freedom.

Three orphaned black bear cubs gain strength and weight in their special enclosure until they can be released back into the wild. (photo by Fffwildlifecenter)

Thinking of becoming a wildlife rehabilitator? You'll need specialized training in wildlife care to learn about handling wild animals, feeding healthy diets, tackling habitat needs, and treating common diseases.

You'll also need licenses issued by the NYS Department of Environmental Conservation (DEC) to work with wild creatures. Why? Native wildlife is considered a natural resource. The creatures of the Catskills belong to everyone living in New York State. Wild animals should never be kept as pets, no matter how tempting. The goal is always to return creatures to the wild, healthy and strong.

Wildlife rehabilitators need other essential skills. As unpaid volunteers, they raise funds to cover expenses. They build safe enclosures to help their wild patients heal. They transport animals to veterinarians for treatment. They serve as "Ambassadors for Wildlife," teaching people how to live peacefully with our wildlife. They think quick on their feet during workdays that can stretch to 14 hours. Finally, they scout out the perfect locations to release Catskill creatures back to their natural habitats.

Most individual wildlife rehabilitators specialize in certain types of species, such as mammals, reptiles, and birds. Click on this website to find a wildlife rehabilitator near you: dec.ny.gov/cfmx/extapps/sls_searches/index.cfm?p=live_rehab

Catskill Wildlife Centers

Friends of the Feathered & Furry Wildlife Center

A thrilling day as Missy releases a bald eagle who made a full recovery from lead poisoning. (photo by Fffwildlifecenter)

Founded by Barbara "Missy" Runyan, FFF's goal is to "let wild be wild." Animals from across New York State arrive at the center where most are rehabilitated and released back to their wild habitats. A sloth of orphaned bear cubs wintered over in large enclosures, gaining weight and tree climbing experience, until they were returned to the forest where they belong. fffwildlifecenter.org

Ellen rescued Rocky and released the famous saw-whet owl after eight days of fluids and a steady diet of mice. (photo by Ravensbeard Wildlife Center)

Ravensbeard Wildlife Center

Ellen Kalish, the founder of Ravensbeard, focuses on native and migratory wild birds. Her wildlife center gained nation attention after rescuing Rocky, a saw-whet owl who stowed away for 170 miles inside the Rockefeller Center Christmas tree. After a week of rehabilitation and a diet of mice, Rocky was released into her native habitat. ravensbeard.org

*Wildlife centers house a variety of native species.
These second chance havens handle, rehabilitate, and release animals
from across New York State. Visit their websites to get involved!*

One of several great horned owls that Annie rehabbed and released. (photo by Annie Mardiney)

TOP LEFT: *Terra, a female American kestrel, is an education bird.* (photo by Erin Archuleta)

TOP CENTER: *While learning to fly, male peregrine falcon Meng hit a box truck on the Mid-Hudson Bridge and became blind in his right eye so he's unreleasable. This raptor was born under the bridge on a platform specifically installed for peregrines, and now stars as an education ambassador.* (photo by Annie Mardiney)

Wild Mountain Birds

Annie Mardiney, founder of Wild Mountain Birds, takes in between 300 to 500 wild birds, including raptors, annually. Many of the birds recuperate in flight buildings before being released into the wild where they have a second chance. About 15 owls, hawks, and falcons who can't be released join educational programs to teach people about feathers, wings, and avian things. wildmountainbirds.com

A ruby-throated humming bird needed to be rehabbed after hitting a window. (photo by Annie Mardiney)

About the Author

Nancy Furstinger has always felt a connection with all creatures great and small, perhaps because her surname (fur + stinger) conjures up images of bears and honeybees. She is the author of nearly 100 books, including many on her favorite topic: animals! She started her writing career in third grade, when her class performed a play she wrote. Since then, Nancy has been a feature writer for a daily newspaper, a managing editor of trade and consumer magazines, and an editor at two children's book publishing houses. She shares her home and heart with her partner plus big dogs, house rabbits, and a chinchilla (all rescued), and volunteers for several animal organizations. Nancy has been speaking up for animals since she learned to talk, and she hasn't shut up yet! Please adopt, don't shop. Learn more at her website: nancyfurstinger.com

Special appreciation to artist extraordinaire Bob Ebdon for his colored pencil illustrations

Bob Ebdon is a retired award-winning artist and musician who specialized in colored pencil work. He lives in Lincoln, United Kingdom, with his wife of fifty years, Gillian.

Sniff Out More: Further Information About Catskill Wildlife

AUDUBON NEW YORK
https://ny.audubon.org/

BAT CONSERVATION INTERNATIONAL
http://www.batcon.org/

BEAVERS: WETLANDS & WILDLIFE
https://www.beaversww.org/

NEW YORK STATE DEPARTMENT OF ENVIRONMENTAL CONSERVATION
https://www.dec.ny.gov/23.html

NORTH AMERICAN BLUEBIRD SOCIETY
http://www.nabluebirdsociety.org

TROUT UNLIMITED http://www.tu.org